What's inside?

See-through pages and magic surprises!

When you see this picture,
hold the page up to the light.

 Thames & Hudson

What's inside this book?

I'm Zim. I'm curious and ask lots of questions.

I'm Zam.
I like finding things out and explaining how things work.

I'm Zoom.
I can change into different shapes.

What's inside your body?

Let's find out
what's inside
your head.

What happens when you grow?

Touch the skin on your arm. Can you feel the muscles and bones underneath? They grow bigger as you grow up.

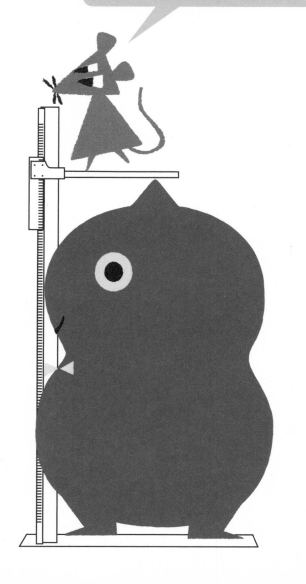

My pyjamas are too small! I must be growing.

Zoom is also growing. Look, he's being measured.

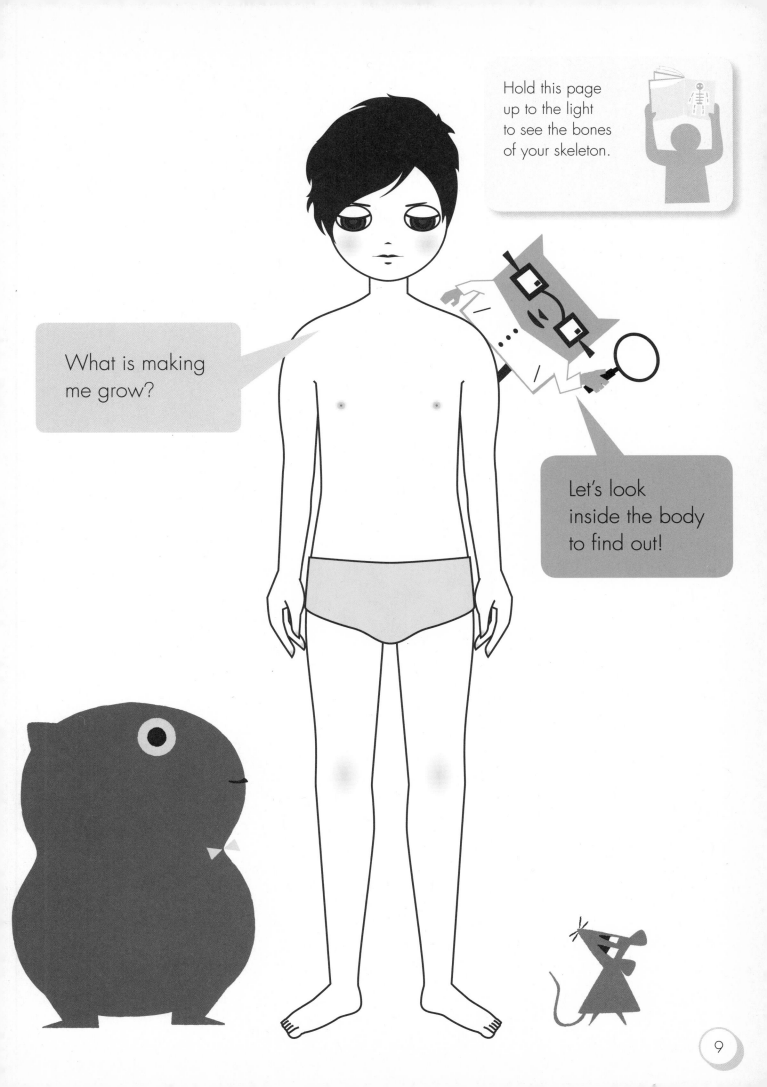

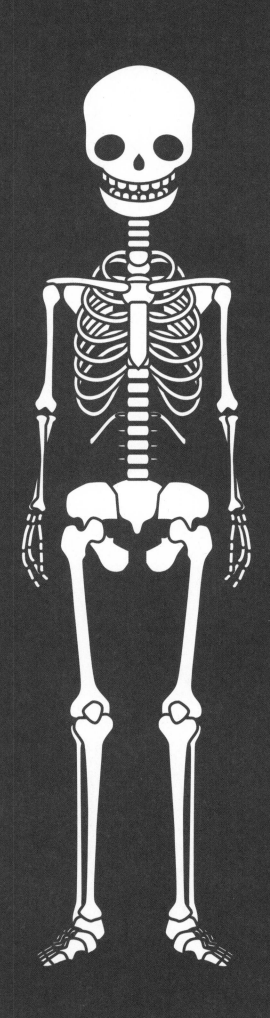

The bones in the body are called a skeleton. As your bones grow, you become taller. Bones help to give you your shape. They also help you to move.

Even when you sleep, your bones are growing. Usually, bones stop growing between the ages of 17 and 20.

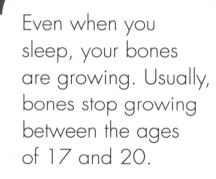

What's inside to make you move?

Jump up and down! Now dance round and round. Go on!
What's happening inside your body when you move?

Do you have cogs
like a wind-up robot?

Do you have strings
like a puppet?

Do you have batteries
like a toy dog?

Hold this page up to the light to see the muscles in your body.

I don't have cogs or strings or batteries, so what's making me move?

Let's look inside the body to find out!

What's inside pulling his arms and legs?

Muscles pull on bones to help us walk, dance and jump!

When you kick a ball or pick up a pencil, a muscle pulls on a bone to make it move. There are over 600 muscles in your body.

There are around 40 muscles in your face.
They help you to smile, frown, look angry and cheeky!

One special muscle moves all the time but you don't notice it. Your heart is a muscle. It pumps blood around your body. Can you feel it beating?

Feel the muscle in the top of your arm. Now lift up your arm. Can you feel the muscle getting bigger? It's pulling your arm up!

Your stomach has muscles that help to squash food. Listen! Can you hear your stomach rumbling?

What happens to food inside your body?

Food goes on a journey inside your body. Let's find out what happens to a plate of delicious lunch.

17

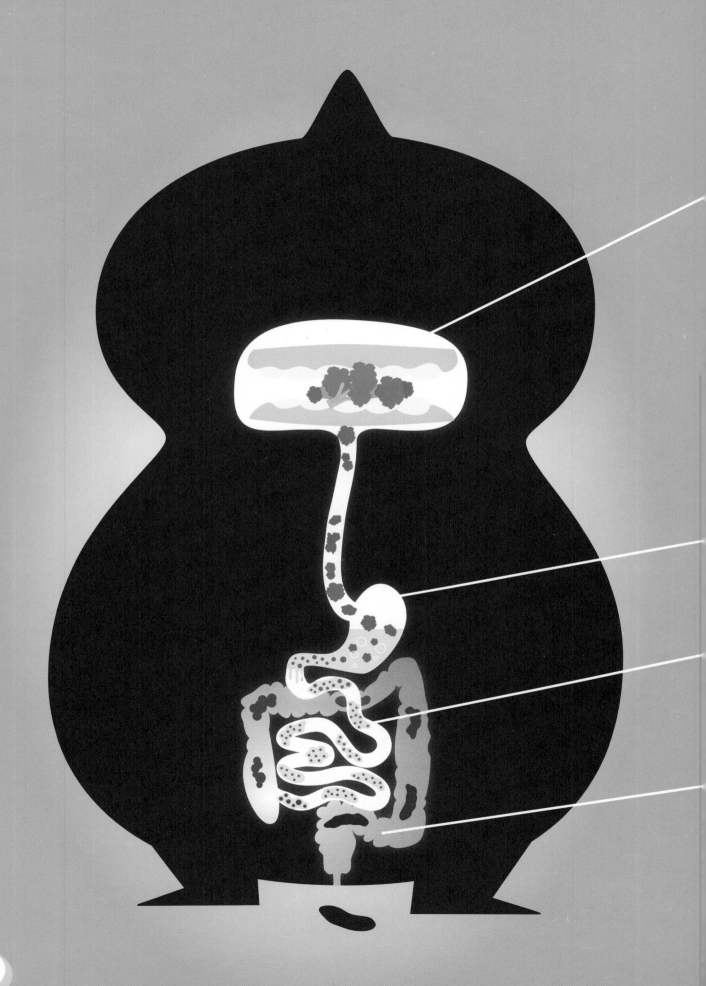

First, we cut and chew the food into small pieces with our teeth. We taste if the food is salty, sweet, bitter or sour with our tongue.

Next we swallow and the pieces go down a long tube!

In the stomach, the food mixes with juices, which break it down into even tinier bits.

These pieces go into a long, wiggly tube called the intestines. Then even tinier bits of food travel in blood around the body.

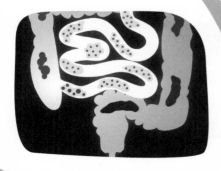

The leftover bits carry on through the tube and come out as poo!

What's inside your head?

Knock knock! What's inside your head? Tap your head gently. Can you feel a big bone? This is your skull. It protects something precious inside your head that helps you to ...

Dream!

Think!

Remember!

Decide what to do next!

See, hear, touch, smell and taste!

Feel happy!

What's doing all these things? Let's look inside the head to find out!

Hold this page up to the light to see the brain inside your head.

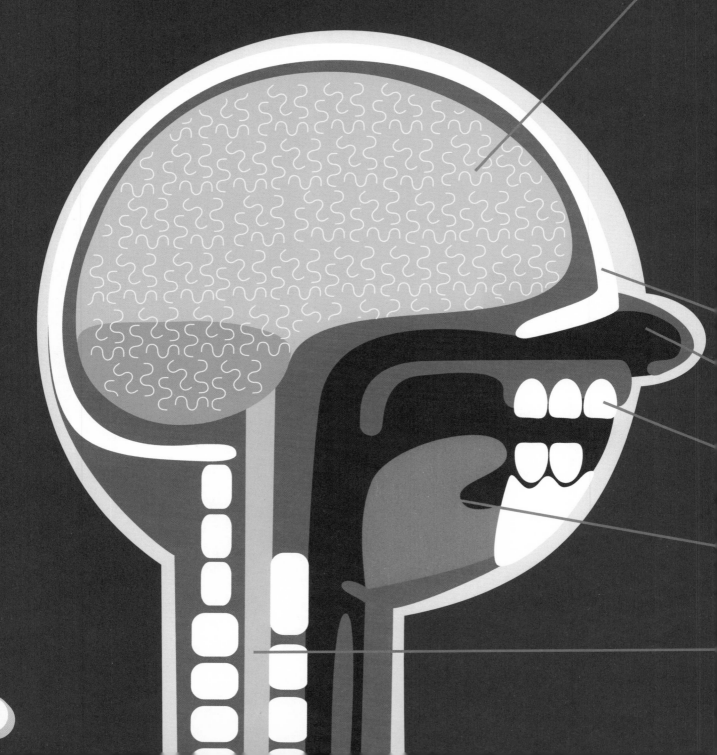

This is the **brain**! It helps you to do all kinds of things! Different parts of the brain control different parts of your body. Which part helps you to hear sounds?

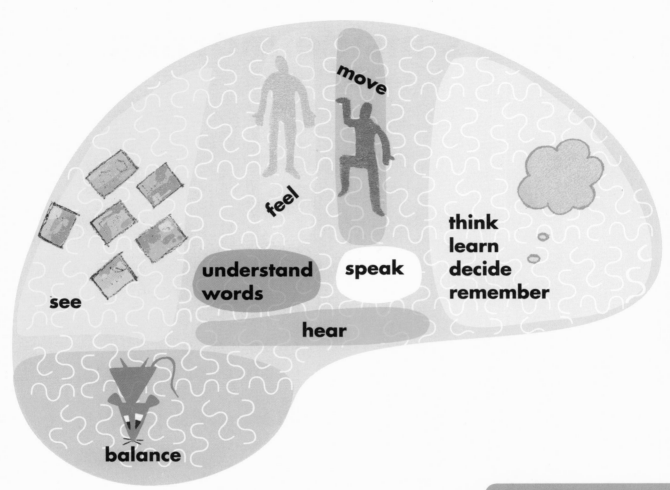

move

feel

see

understand words

speak

hear

think
learn
decide
remember

balance

Your **skull** is a hollow bone that protects your brain. It's just like a hard box.

Your **nose** helps you to smell things.

Teeth inside your mouth help you to chew food.

When you talk, you move your **tongue**. It also helps you to taste your food.

All day long, messages travel from your **brain** along the **spinal cord** to different parts of the body to make it do things.

Wow! There's lots going on inside my head!

23

What's inside machines?

What's inside a robot? I've got a friend who's a robot.

Tick tock! I can hear a clock ticking. What's inside a clock?

What's inside a robot?

Are you a living thing or a robot? Zoom is a living thing, just like you. OK-1 is a robot, who is asking some rather odd questions ...

Hold the page up to the light to see what's inside Zoom and robot OK-1.

Zoom

ROBOT OK-1

Let's take a look inside Zoom and OK-1.

These are the differences between a robot and a living thing.

Robot

OK-1 has a light flashing on top of its head. It's how you know it's switched on.

OK-1 has a battery to give it energy.

OK-1 has circuits and microchips to send signals to control its body.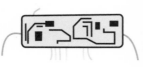

OK-1 has cogs and a winch to lift its legs and arms.

Zoom's stomach helps him break down his lunch to release the energy inside the food.

Zoom

Zoom has a brain that sends messages to control his body.

Zoom has a heart to pump blood around his body to keep him warm and nourished. His heart pumps all the time.

Zoom has muscles and bones to help him move about.

Can you see the differences?

What's inside a rocket?

Let's find out what's inside a rocket. How can it fly so far into space? It's time to go to the Moon. Whoosh!

Zam, I want to go to the Moon. How will we get there?

Hmm …
I could turn into a rocket.

Well, Zim.
We need a rocket.

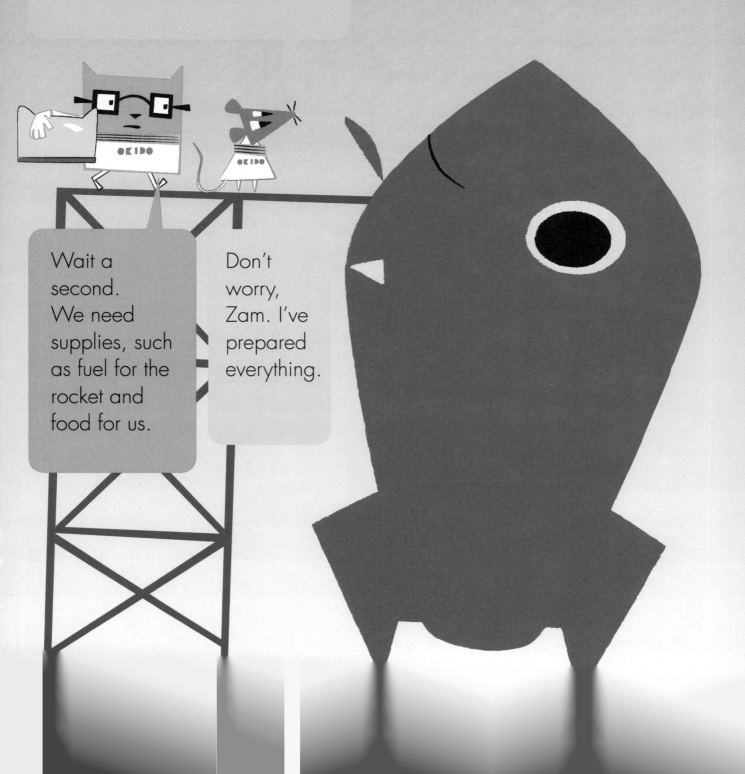

Hold this page up to the light to see inside the rocket!

Wow! Zoom, that's amazing! You've turned into a real rocket.

Wait a second. We need supplies, such as fuel for the rocket and food for us.

Don't worry, Zam. I've prepared everything.

The rocket needs energy from fuel to lift off.
In space the rocket travels around Earth,
the Moon and other planets.

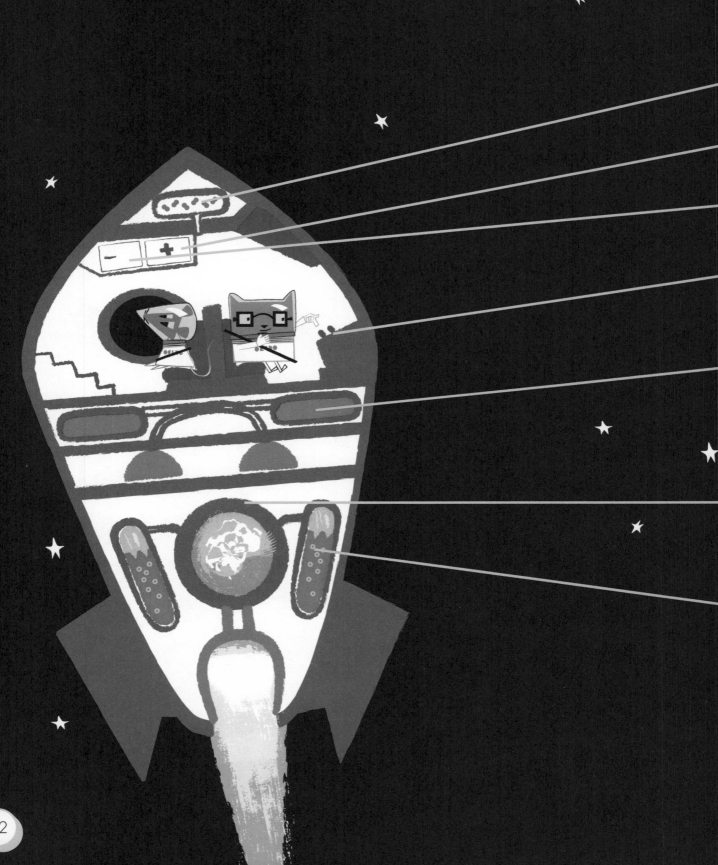

oxygen tank
so Zim and Zam
can breathe.

first aid

food storage

control panel

**secondary
fuel tanks**

rocket engine

**primary
fuel tanks**

Look Zim, the Earth
seems so small
from up here!

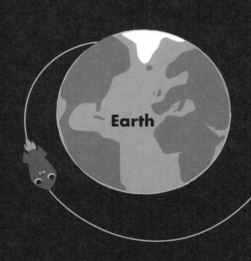

Moon

Earth

We're
approaching
the Moon,
Zoom. Prepare
for landing …

What's inside a car?

Zim, Zam and Zoom are driving their cars.
Let's find out what makes cars move!

Hold this page up to the light to see inside the car.

Let's look under the bonnet to find out.

The **engine** burns fuel to power the car and make it go.

The **battery** lights up the indicators and the dashboard display.

When it's dark, Zim puts on the. **headlights** to help her see.

The **accelerator** makes the car travel faster.

The **steering wheel** is connected to the wheels to turn the car left and right.

The **exhaust pipe** takes away nasty fumes.

The **radiator** cools the engine down so it doesn't get too hot.

The **brake pedal** makes the wheels slow down. Press it harder and it stops the car.

What's inside an alarm clock?

A clock tells us the time.

The big hand is on the 12. The little hand is on the 9. It's 9 o'clock!

How does a clock do that? And how does it know when to wake you up in the morning?

Tick tock! Let's look inside to see what makes the hands move!

Hold this page up to the light to see inside the clock!

It's evening, and Zoom is winding his alarm clock. He needs to wake up early in the morning!

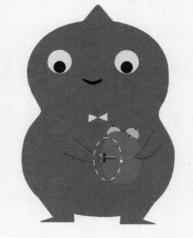

First the key winds up a spring inside the clock. As the spring slowly unwinds, it turns a cog, which turns more cogs.

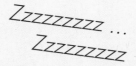
Zzzzzzzz ...
Zzzzzzzz

During the night, one of the cogs turns the hands on the clock's face.

Aaargh!

Brrrringgg!

In the morning, when the hands reach the set time, they trigger a striker to ring the bells. Zoom! Time to wake up!

What's inside the world of nature?

What lives inside a tree, and what's beneath our feet?

What can you find in a cave, and what's inside a huge whale?

What's inside a tree?

Zim, Zam and Zoom are in the forest.
They can hear birds singing but can't see them.
Where are the birds?

Look at the
tall trees.

I wonder
who lives
at the top?

Hold this page up to the light to see inside the tree!

Let's go inside and find out!

A tree is home to many kinds of animals, including lots of birds.

A **bird** makes a nest out of twigs and leaves. The nest protects the eggs and babies.

An **owl** makes its nest inside a hole in a tree trunk. It sleeps during the day and flies at night to hunt for food.

A **squirrel** also makes a nest in the branches. It stores nuts to eat in winter.

Creepy crawlies, such as ladybirds, spiders and ants, live on the rough bark.

Did you know that different birds sing different songs?

What's inside a whale?

Look, it's a whale! Is a whale a huge fish?
No, it's a mammal. You're a mammal, too!

Hold this page up to the light to see inside the whale.

Well, let's find out! What's inside a whale?

Whales like this one are the largest kind of animal on our planet.

Whales breathe air. That's why they come to the surface. Before they take a new breath, they need to blow out first.

Some whales eat fish, crabs and squid. Others eat lots of tiny sea creatures.

The whale has a skeleton made of bones, just like you!

What's under the ground?

What do you think you would find if you dug into the ground? Apart from mud and rocks, what else is there under our feet?

There is a pond here too! What lives under the water?

The rabbit lives underground. What other animals do too?

Let's go underground and find out!

Hold this page
up to the light
to see under
the ground.

Worms and insects live in the soil. There's another world under your feet!

The roots of trees and plants grow underground. Roots suck up water and goodness from soil to help the plants grow.

Rabbits and other animals live in burrows underground.

What's inside a cave?

Zim has found a rocky cave.
It was formed thousands of years ago.
Do you think it's empty?

Brrr! I'm cold out here. It looks warm and snug inside.

But it's dark. Do you think anything lives in there?

Let's look inside to find out.

Hold this page
up to the light
to see inside
the cave.

Shh! A **bear** is asleep inside the cave. In winter, a bear goes to sleep for a long time to keep warm and save energy.

Long ago, prehistoric people lived in this cave and drew pictures on the walls. These are called **cave paintings**.

There are bones in the ground! When animals or plants die, their remains may get buried in the ground and preserved as **fossils**.

Long thin bits of rock hanging from the ceiling of a cave are called **stalactites**. They form from drips of water over many years.

It is spring and the **bear** has woken up. She's going outside to find some food!

What's inside buildings?

Do you live in a house or a tall block of flats?

Have you ever been inside a castle?

What happens inside a theatre? Let's look inside buildings!

What's inside a house?

Zim, Zam and Zoom are walking down the street.
What is happening behind the doors of the houses they pass?

I wonder who lives inside this big pink house?

We could ring the doorbell …

Yes! let's find out.

Hold this page up to the light to see inside a house.

63

A family lives inside the house. They are doing different things in different rooms.

In one **bedroom**, a child is playing before going to bed. How many bedrooms can you count?

Who is in the **living room**? What are they doing today?

Which pet animal is playing in the **attic**?

Which rooms does your home have?

What's inside a skyscraper?

A really tall building is called a skyscraper. Skyscrapers reach up high into the sky.

Look at all those windows! I wonder what's inside?

Hold this page up to the light to see inside a skyscraper.

Wow! This is the top of the skyscraper.

There are many floors of offices and workrooms below. People live and work in the skyscraper.

Who's waiting for the lift? Which floor number is the lift on at the moment?

Can you find the water tank?

How many computers are there?

What do you think is in the box that the man is delivering on the 6th floor?

Hey! Keep the noise down, you lot!

Look at all the wires! Which machines do the wires connect to the power supply?

What's inside a castle?

Long ago, a king and queen and all their knights
and ladies lived in a big castle with thick stone walls.

Hold this page up to the light to see inside a castle.

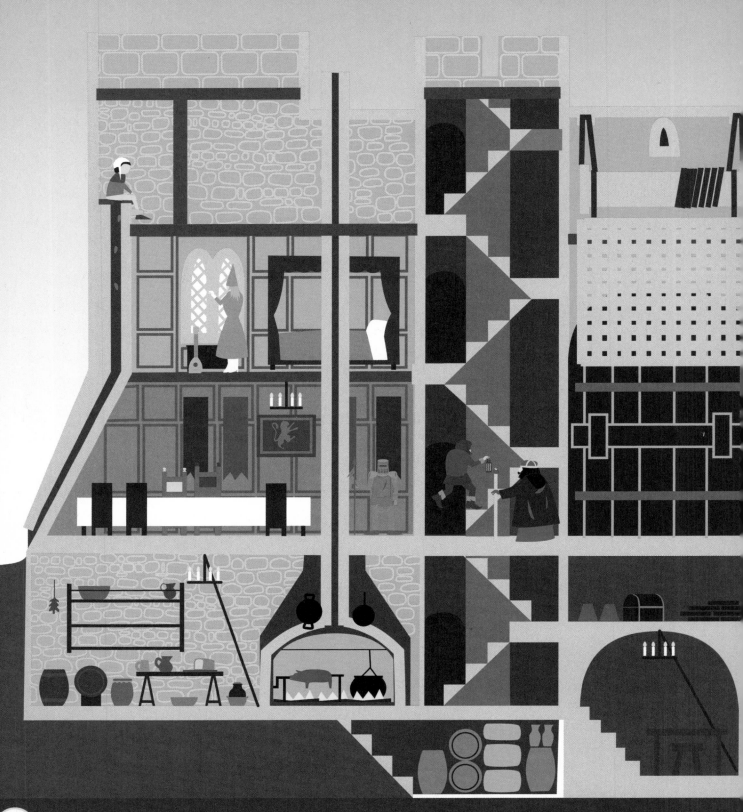

Who do you think sleeps in the **royal bedchamber**, on a big bed with four posts and curtains?

Watch out! The **portcullis** is coming down. It's a heavy metal gate that protects the front door of the castle.

Which animal is being roasted on a spit in the castle **kitchen**?

Who eats dinner in the **great hall** with the king and queen?

Where do the knights keep their swords and suits of armour? It's called an **armoury**.

The king keeps prisoners locked in the **dungeon**. They get only bread and water to eat.

Can you spot the supplies of wine and grain in the cold, dark **cellar**?

I'm king of the castle!

What's inside a theatre?

We're at the theatre. The show is about to start. We must be quiet!

I can hear an orchestra getting ready, but where are they?

Shh! Let's find out what's behind the red curtain.

Hold this page up to the light to see inside a theatre.

Curtains up! Everyone backstage has a job to do.

What will happen when the **stagehand** in blue overalls pulls the rope?

Who is shining the **spotlights** at the actor on stage?

Who is in the **prop room** waiting for a fake sword?

How many musicians in the **orchestra pit** are playing violins?

Can you see the **dressing rooms**? What happens to the actors there?

It's your turn!

Have fun! On these pages
you can draw what's inside.

You will need to turn
the page first ...

... and when you see
this pencil, you can
draw on the page!

Finally, turn back
the page to see the
present you've put
inside the box.

What's inside this box?

Turn the page and draw a picture. Then hold this page up to the light.

79

Draw a present inside this white space. Now turn back the page to see your present inside the box.

What's inside the fridge?

Turn the page and draw a picture. Then hold this page up to the light.

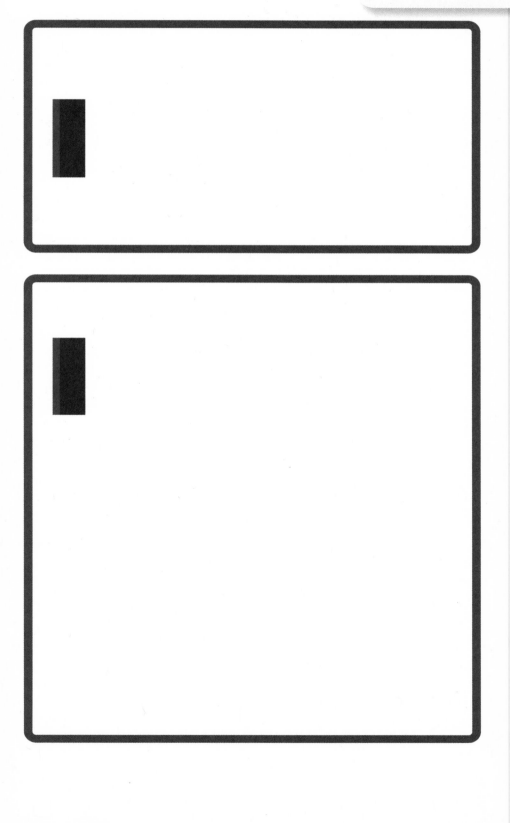

Fill up the fridge with your favourite foods. Now turn back to see your food inside the fridge.

Who's behind this door?

Turn the page
and draw a picture.
Then hold this page
up to the light.

Draw a mystery guest in the doorway. Now turn back to see who's behind the door!

What's inside this tree?

Turn the page and draw a picture. Then hold this page up to the light.

85

Draw lots of living creatures in this tree.
Now turn back to see them through
the branches.

What's under the hand?

Turn the page and draw a picture. Then hold this page up to the light.

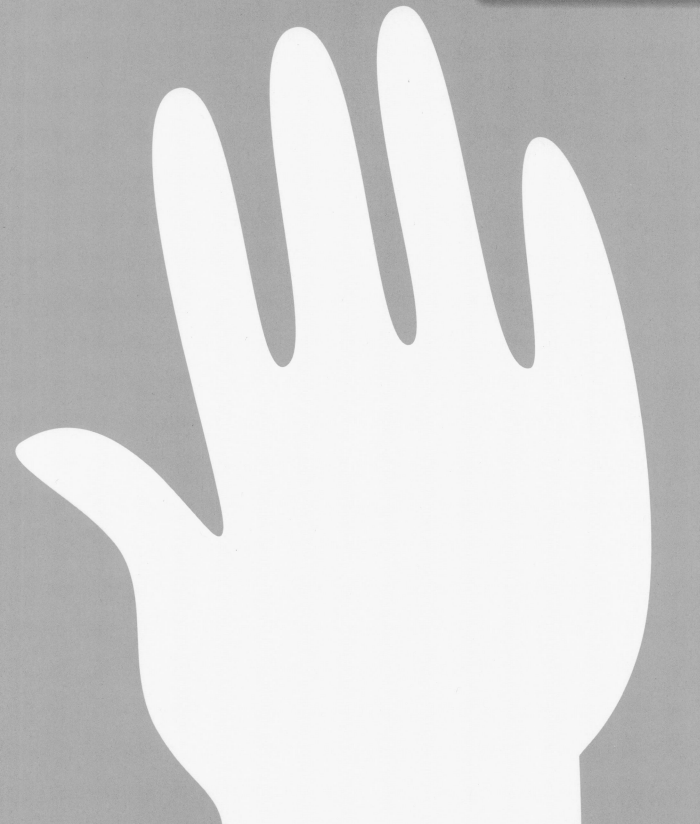

87

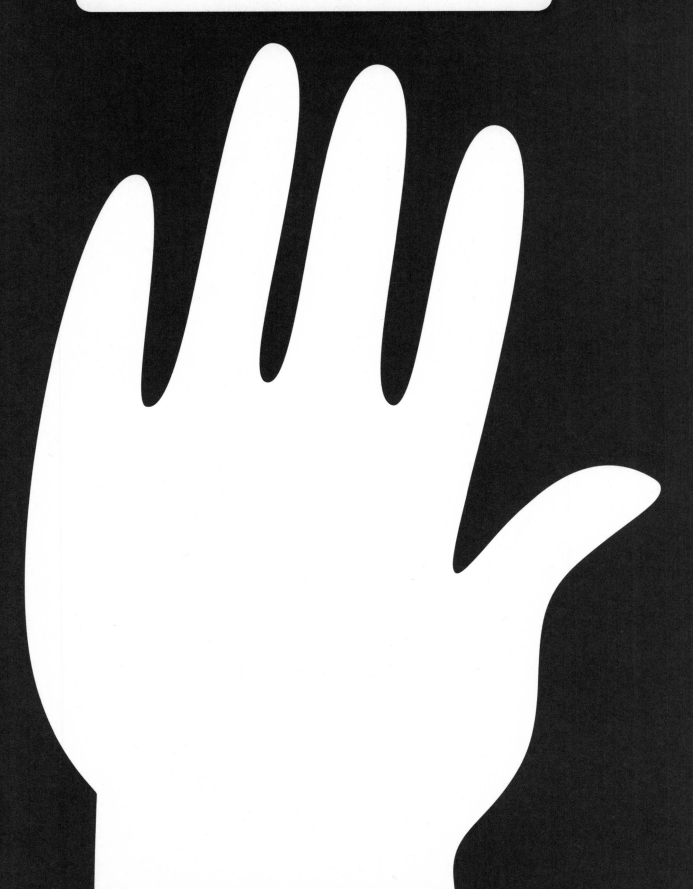

Draw what's under the hand. Now turn back to see what you've drawn.

What's inside this chocolate egg?

Turn the page and draw a picture. Then hold this page up to the light.

89

What would you like to find in this chocolate egg? Draw it and then turn back to see inside the egg.

What's inside this removal truck?

Turn the page and draw a picture. Then hold this page up to the light.

You're moving house. Draw what's in the truck and draw yourself as the driver too! Now turn back to see inside the truck.

What's inside this toy cupboard?

Turn the page and draw a picture. Then hold this page up to the light.

Fill up the cupboard with amazing toys.
Now turn back to see the toys inside
the cupboard.

Bye for now!
You've come to the
end of the book!

Do you want to
start again from
the beginning?

Or perhaps you could
guess what's inside the
things around you and
draw them!

First published in the United Kingdom in 2013 by
Thames & Hudson Ltd, 181A High Holborn, London WC1V 7QX

What's inside? © 2013 OKIDO

OKIDO Studio
the arts and science magazine for kids
okido.co.uk

Concept and design by Sophie Dauvois
Illustrations by Alex Barrow, Maggie Li,
Mathilde Nivet and Acacio Ortas
Additional illustrations by Kaz Takahashi

British Library Cataloguing-in-Publication Data

A catalogue record for this book is available
from the British Library

ISBN 978-0-500-65019-6

Printed and bound in China by Toppan Leefung

To find out about all our publications, please visit
www.thamesandhudson.com. There you can subscribe
to our e-newsletter, browse or download our current
catalogue, and buy any titles that are in print.